The Donkey and the Golden Light

by JOHN AND GILL SPEIRS

HARRY N. ABRAMS, INC., PUBLISHERS

ong ago, in a stable behind an inn, a donkey was born. Shepherds crowded into the small space. They helped the donkey take his first steps.

"We'll call him Bethlehem, after this town!" they said. An angel had appeared to them and had led them from their flocks on the hillside to the stable.

Kings in fine robes knelt before a young woman, Mary, and her baby, Jesus. They laid precious gifts at their feet. Mary's husband, Joseph, and the shepherds looked on in adoration.

The brightest star that ever shone led the kings to this place. It filled the heavens with magnificent golden light as choirs of angels proclaimed peace, goodwill, and a new beginning for all.

The little family was warned of great danger for baby boys. Frosty winds chased them on their sudden, secret flight from the stable. The cry of warning bells across the icy air hurried them out of town at the start of their long and perilous journey to far distant lands.

The stable, shepherds, richly dressed kings, the magnificent golden light—all became muddled together in Bethlehem's mind as he kept close to his mother's side on this desperate search for safety.

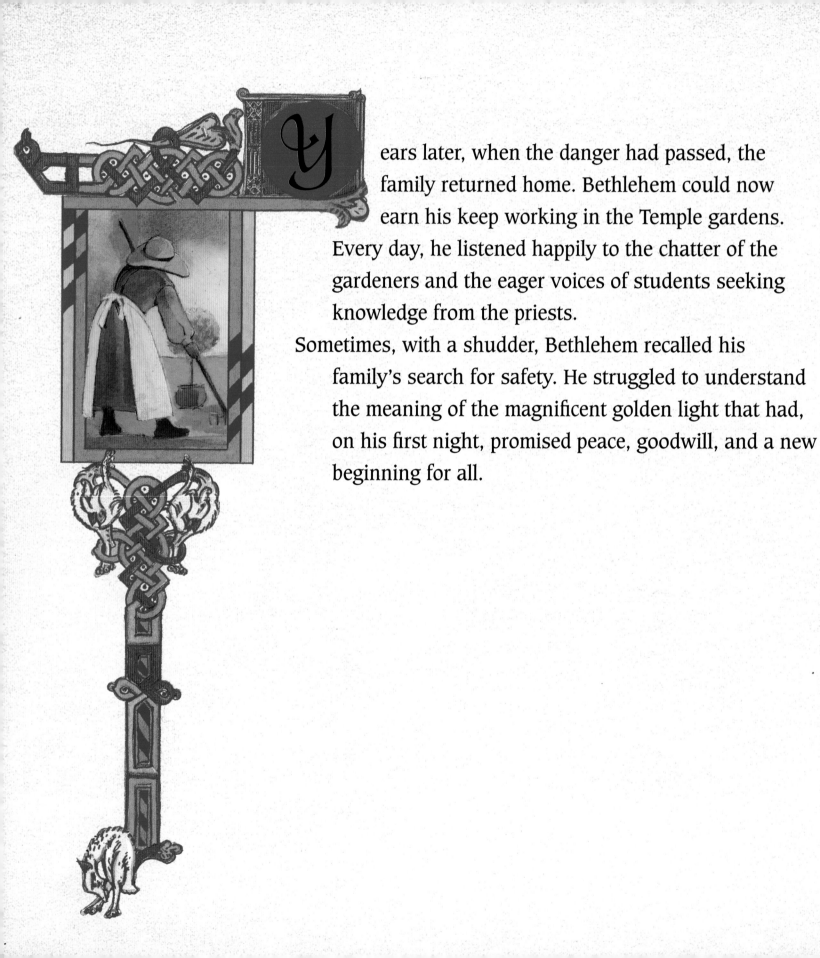

Years later, when the danger had passed, the family returned home. Bethlehem could now earn his keep working in the Temple gardens. Every day, he listened happily to the chatter of the gardeners and the eager voices of students seeking knowledge from the priests.

Sometimes, with a shudder, Bethlehem recalled his family's search for safety. He struggled to understand the meaning of the magnificent golden light that had, on his first night, promised peace, goodwill, and a new beginning for all.

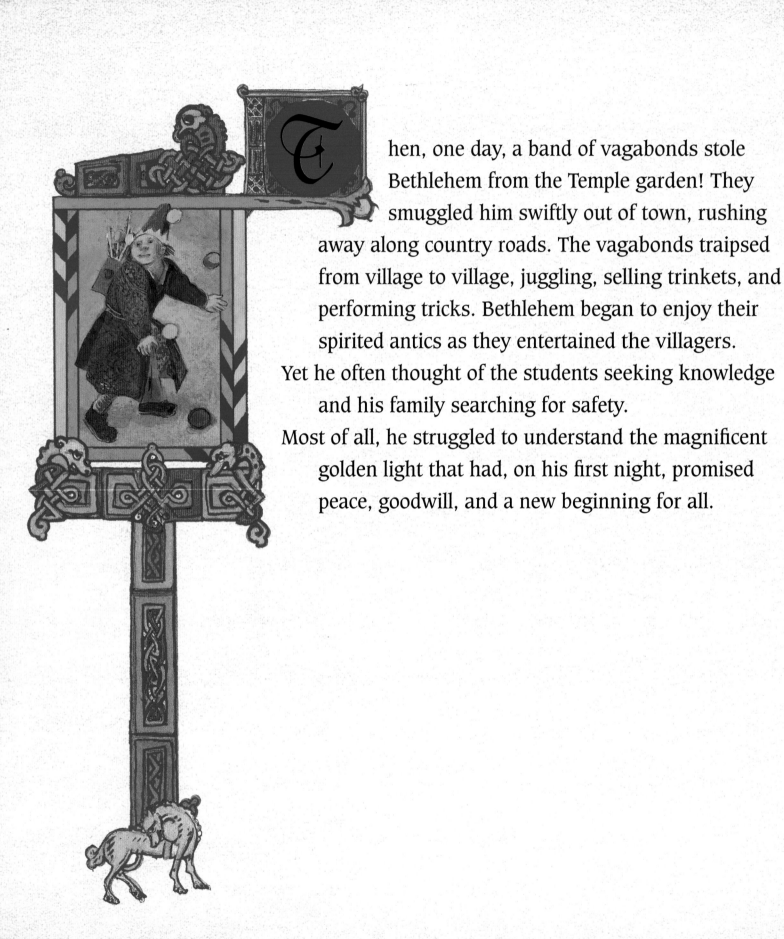

hen, one day, a band of vagabonds stole Bethlehem from the Temple garden! They smuggled him swiftly out of town, rushing away along country roads. The vagabonds traipsed from village to village, juggling, selling trinkets, and performing tricks. Bethlehem began to enjoy their spirited antics as they entertained the villagers.

Yet he often thought of the students seeking knowledge and his family searching for safety.

Most of all, he struggled to understand the magnificent golden light that had, on his first night, promised peace, goodwill, and a new beginning for all.

One day the vagabonds met a merchant caravan and bartered Bethlehem away for bales of bright silks. The merchants were honest but ambitious in their pursuit of riches. Horses and camels with their swaying loads jostled Bethlehem as he clambered up and down the mountain paths. From city to city, town to town, a hundred tramping feet stirred up the rocky ground, filling Bethlehem's eyes and mouth with gritty dust.

As he trudged along, Bethlehem thought back to the vagabonds entertaining the villagers, the students seeking knowledge, and his family searching for safety.

Still he struggled to understand the magnificent golden light that had, on his first night, promised peace, goodwill, and a new beginning for all.

hen the merchants had no more use for
Bethlehem, he was sold to a kindly farmer who
needed him to work the land. Bethlehem,
hauling in the sheaves of wheat, heard the peasants'
songs drifting down the hill and across the golden
fields. They celebrated the harvest and hoped for a
bountiful future.

He thought of the merchants pursuing riches,
the vagabonds entertaining the villagers,
the students seeking knowledge,
and his family searching for safety.

Still he struggled to understand the magnificent golden
light that had, on his first night, promised peace,
goodwill, and a new beginning for all.

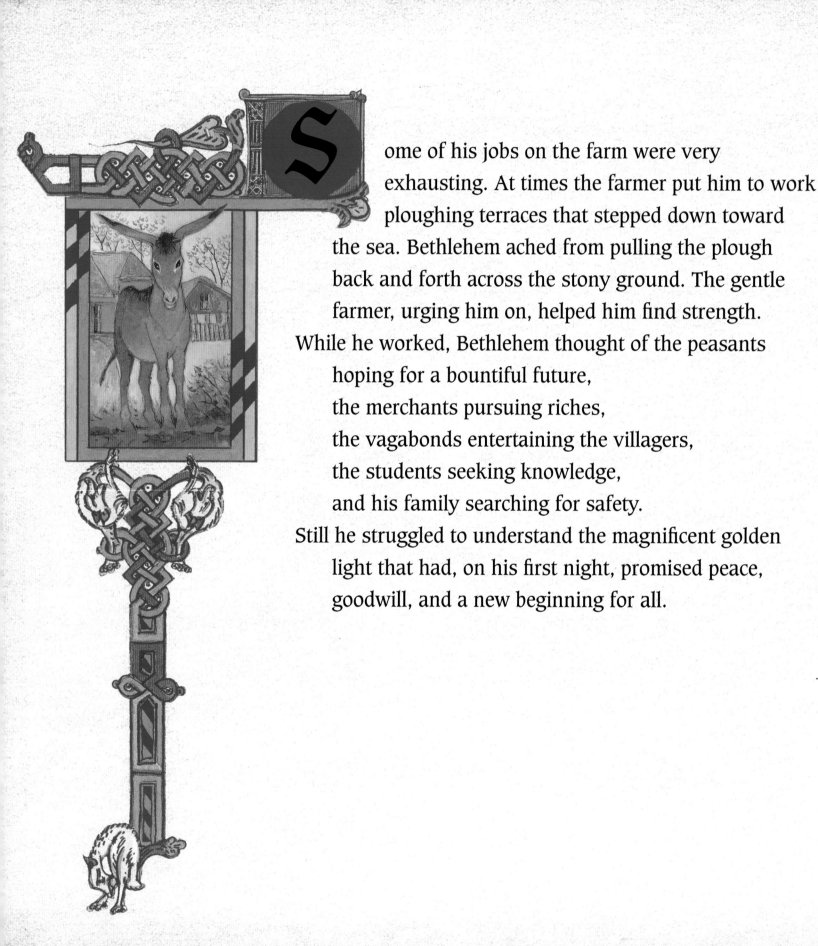

ome of his jobs on the farm were very
exhausting. At times the farmer put him to work
ploughing terraces that stepped down toward
the sea. Bethlehem ached from pulling the plough
back and forth across the stony ground. The gentle
farmer, urging him on, helped him find strength.
While he worked, Bethlehem thought of the peasants
hoping for a bountiful future,
the merchants pursuing riches,
the vagabonds entertaining the villagers,
the students seeking knowledge,
and his family searching for safety.
Still he struggled to understand the magnificent golden
light that had, on his first night, promised peace,
goodwill, and a new beginning for all.

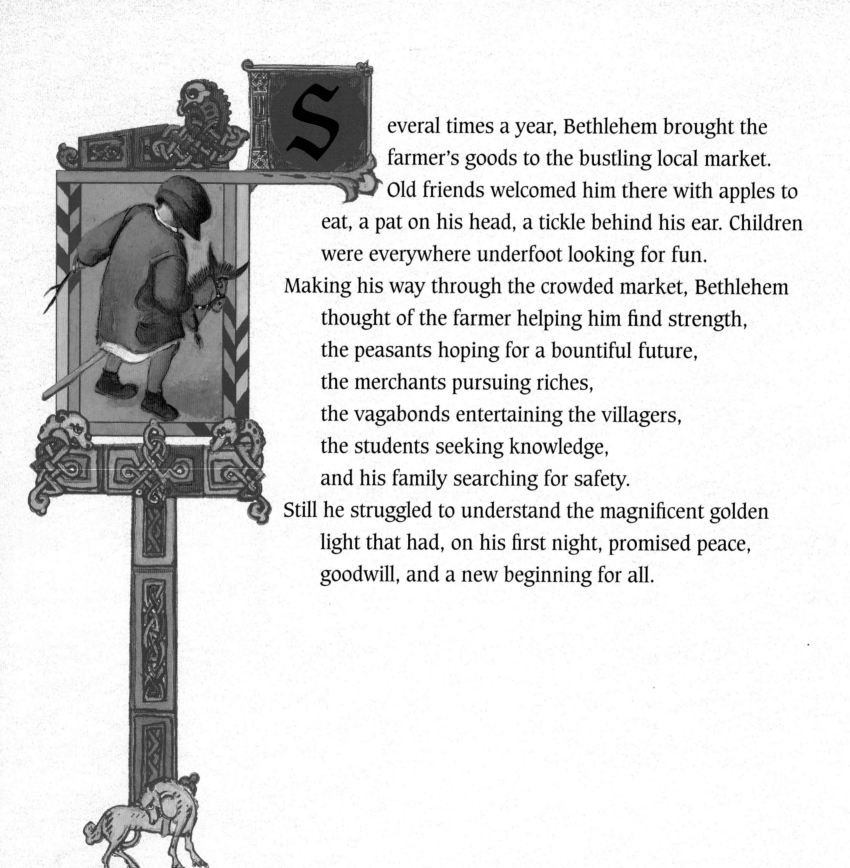

Several times a year, Bethlehem brought the
farmer's goods to the bustling local market.
Old friends welcomed him there with apples to
eat, a pat on his head, a tickle behind his ear. Children
were everywhere underfoot looking for fun.
Making his way through the crowded market, Bethlehem
thought of the farmer helping him find strength,
the peasants hoping for a bountiful future,
the merchants pursuing riches,
the vagabonds entertaining the villagers,
the students seeking knowledge,
and his family searching for safety.
Still he struggled to understand the magnificent golden
light that had, on his first night, promised peace,
goodwill, and a new beginning for all.

As the days grew shorter and the air colder, Bethlehem was borrowed by woodcutters. He helped them gather and move wood around the forest floor as they struggled to make a living. He loved to breathe in the smell of damp leaves mingling with the smoke from the fires.

Deep in the forest, Bethlehem thought of the
village children looking for fun,
the farmer helping him find strength,
the peasants hoping for a bountiful future,
the merchants pursuing riches,
the vagabonds entertaining the villagers,
the students seeking knowledge,
and his family searching for safety.

Still he struggled to understand the magnificent golden
light that had, on his first night, promised peace,
goodwill, and a new beginning for all.

fter a bitter winter the farmer was forced to sell
Bethlehem to drovers. These men went far and
wide collecting donkeys, gradually making their
way toward Jerusalem. Bethlehem's future was
uncertain, but he had the company of other donkeys
once again. They comforted one another amidst the
snow and the lashings of the drovers' whips.
As he trod along, Bethlehem thought back to the
   woodcutters struggling to make a living,
   the village children looking for fun,
   the farmer helping him find strength,
   the peasants hoping for a bountiful future,
   the merchants pursuing riches,
   the vagabonds entertaining the villagers,
   the students seeking knowledge,
   and his family searching for safety.
Still he struggled to understand the magnificent golden
   light that had, on his first night, promised peace,
   goodwill, and a new beginning for all.

O utside Jerusalem a group of men persuaded the drovers to give Bethlehem to them. These men wanted the donkey to carry someone into the city. A quiet, gentle man was brought forward, and Bethlehem was puzzled. Didn't he know this man?

Soon crowds surrounded Bethlehem, shouting praises, "Hosanna! Hosanna!" Cheering and laughing, many tore branches from palms. Some waved them like banners; others laid them as a carpet along the path. Bethlehem was confused. Why did they hail this man as a king?

As he made his way into the city, Bethlehem thought of
the donkeys seeking comfort in one another,
the woodcutters struggling to make a living,
the village children looking for fun,
the farmer helping him find strength,
the peasants hoping for a bountiful future,
the merchants pursuing riches,
the vagabonds entertaining the villagers,
the students seeking knowledge,
and his family searching for safety.

Still he struggled to understand the magnificent golden light that had, on his first night, promised peace, goodwill, and a new beginning for all.

ater the city grew chilly and still. Bethlehem, forgotten by the crowds, wandered aimlessly through empty streets. His tired legs reminded him that he had grown old. And he was all alone.

He yearned for the crowds shouting "Hosanna,"
the donkeys seeking comfort in one another,
the woodcutters struggling to make a living,
the village children looking for fun,
the farmer helping him find strength,
the peasants hoping for a bountiful future,
the merchants pursuing riches,
the vagabonds entertaining the villagers,
the students seeking knowledge,
and his family searching for safety.

Still he struggled to understand the magnificent golden light that had, on his first night, promised peace, goodwill, and a new beginning for all.

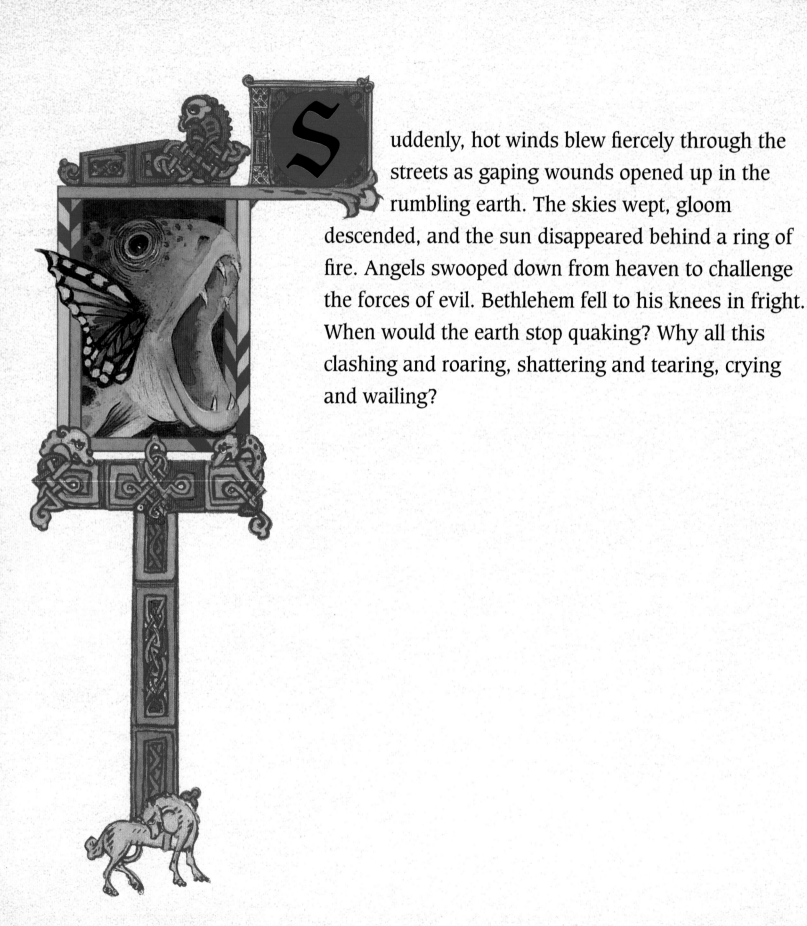

Suddenly, hot winds blew fiercely through the streets as gaping wounds opened up in the rumbling earth. The skies wept, gloom descended, and the sun disappeared behind a ring of fire. Angels swooped down from heaven to challenge the forces of evil. Bethlehem fell to his knees in fright. When would the earth stop quaking? Why all this clashing and roaring, shattering and tearing, crying and wailing?

ith aching heart and limbs, Bethlehem stumbled out of the desolate city and came upon a gardener. Bethlehem could go no further.

He remembered all the events and people from his life:

the crowds crying "Hosanna,"

the donkeys seeking comfort in one another,

the woodcutters struggling to make a living,

the village children looking for fun,

the farmer helping him find strength,

the peasants hoping for a bountiful future,

the merchants pursuing riches,

the vagabonds entertaining the villagers,

the students seeking knowledge,

and his family searching for safety.

Suddenly, Bethlehem was suffused in magnificent golden light. He recognized it at once: a child had been born on the same night as he, and with this child came shepherds, kings, and this magnificent light. That child was now the man before him and the man Bethlehem had carried so proudly into the city.

The gardener smiled and opened His arms. The donkey's sadness, pain, and weariness left him. With joy, Bethlehem went to Him and His promise of peace, goodwill, and a new beginning for all.

Illustration References

Each story painting is 12 x 11 inches (30 x 28 cm). The smaller paintings are each approximately 3 x 5 inches (9 x 12 cm). The details below are from the story paintings, in consecutive book order. Each detail portrays a different period in Jesus' life. Beside each detail, the stage of Jesus' life is given. Also provided is the title of the story painting and the title of the painting by Pieter Bruegel the Elder (and its current locale) that inspired the book illustrations. Along with actual paintings, John Speirs also referred to various drawings by Bruegel (see Artist's Note).

The Nativity

Bethlehem Is Born
Inspired by *The Adoration of the Magi*,
National Gallery, London

The Wedding Feast at Cana

Country Wedding/Harvest
Inspired by *The Harvest*,
The Metropolitan Museum of Art, New York

The Flight into Egypt

Through the Snow
Inspired by *The Census at Bethlehem*,
Musées royaux des Beaux-Arts de
Belgique, Brussels

Walking on Water

Ploughing the Fields
Inspired by *The Fall of Icarus*,
Musées royaux des Beaux-Arts de
Belgique, Brussels

The Child Jesus in the Temple

In the Temple Gardens
Inspired by *Spring*, Graphische
Sammlung Albertina, Vienna

Blessing the Children

Market in the Town
Inspired by *Flemish Proverbs*,
Staatliche Museen, Berlin

The Baptism of Jesus

With the Vagabonds
Inspired by *The Battle of Carnival and
Lent*, Kunsthistoriches Museum, Vienna

The Raising of Lazarus

The Woodcutters .
Inspired by *The Return of the Herd*,
Kunsthistoriches Museum, Vienna

Forty Days in the Wilderness/
The Temptation

With the Merchant Caravan
Inspired by *The Conversion of St. Paul*,
Kunsthistoriches Museum, Vienna

Sermon on the Mount

Donkey Drove
Inspired by *Hunters in the Snow*,
or *The Return of the Hunters*,
Kunsthistoriches Museum, Vienna

Entry into Jerusalem

Carrying Jesus
Inspired by *Kermis at Hoboken*,
Courtauld Institute of Art, London

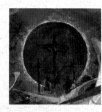

The Crucifixion

Fire All Around
Inspired by *The Fall of the Rebel Angels*,
Musées royaux des Beaux-Arts de
Belgique, Brussels

The Last Supper

Alone in the City
Inspired by *Children's Games*,
Kunsthistoriches Museum, Vienna

The Resurrection

Bethlehem Meets the Gardener
Inspired by *The Procession to Calvary*,
Kunsthistoriches Museum, Vienna

Artist's Note

Similar to my illustrations for *The Little Boy's Christmas Gift*, I have called upon my knowledge of and love for fifteenth- and sixteenth-century European artists, especially the Flemish artist Pieter Bruegel the Elder (1525–1569), for inspiration to produce this series of paintings. These artists depicted Bible stories as set in their own time—incorporating contemporary clothing, buildings, and symbols. I have also used another device of the period—that of paralleling the life of Jesus Christ with the seasons and labors of the months—and taken it a step further by adding another layer: the life of the donkey, Bethlehem, which begins and ends with the life of Jesus. For the years in between, the text deals only with the donkey's life, but important stages in the life of Christ are represented in the background. This too was a device familiar to Bruegel who utilized it in his painting *Landscape with the Parable of the Sower* where, in a tiny detail in the background of the painting, Jesus is shown preaching to a crowd on the banks of a river.

Two of my illustrations, *With the Vagabonds* and *Fire All Around*, contain elements that may appear strange to today's readers. In *With the Vagabonds* there are figures wearing white net cloths over their faces and eggs around their necks. These characters are "Mummers"—bands of players, musicians, and vagabonds—who from the eleventh century through to the seventeenth were a standard element in revels and carnivals. The precise meaning of their costumes is unknown. *Fire All Around* has numerous examples of monsters in the form of fish. This is how Bruegel chose to depict the fallen angels. He was using a recognized symbolism but may also have been influenced by the altarpiece *The Last Judgement* by the artist Hieronymus Bosch.

My wife Gill, who wrote the text, and I have been asked why we chose a donkey as the main character. The legend of how the donkey got its cross—the dark marks that line its back and shoulders—has always intrigued us. There are several versions of the story, none of which are retold in this book. Instead it is the symbol of the donkey, an animal who carries the burdens of others, that we believed was most pertinent. It is said that the donkey has worn this cross since the day it bore Jesus through the streets of Jerusalem.

—John Speirs

WITH THANKS TO TRELD PELKEY BICKNELL AND DENNIS WOODMAN FOR ALL HER HELP AND ENCOURAGEMENT, HOWARD W. REEVES, LINAS ALSENAS, BECKY TERHUNE, AND CELINA CARVALHO AT HARRY N. ABRAMS INC., AND KATHY MASSARO FOR THE GOLDEN LIGHT.

Designer: Celina Carvalho

Library of Congress Cataloging-in-Publication data has been applied for.
ISBN: 0-8109-4812-5

Printed and bound in the U.S.A.
10 9 8 7 6 5 4 3 2 1

Harry N. Abrams, Inc.
100 Fifth Avenue
New York, N.Y. 10011
www.abramsbooks.com

Abrams is a subsidiary of

LA MARTINIÈRE
GROUPE